# A Month That Matters

## 31 Evangelical Essays and Prayers

## By L. R. Abbott

## <u>DEDICATION</u>

To Nathan, Tiffany and Thadd

No one loves you more than Jesus,

and your mother and I both tie for second.

# INTRODUCTION

Here is my challenge to you, my reader. In this book are 31 devotional thoughts culled from matters of life that have come to my attention. There are enough of them to cover any one month of the year. You choose the month that suits your schedule and take one essay a day to read. If at the end of the first week you are disinterested to read the rest of the book, inform me and I will refund you the purchase price no questions asked. I only request you inform me you passed the book on to another person so that they could give it a try.

I think you will find things that you identify with and which are useful to you within these pages. We are not so different you and I. Though we may have never met, though we may never meet, we are people with a shared humanity. This means we've more in common than not and we can connect anywhere and any place if given opportunity. This is that time. This is that place. This book is where you and I meet. I trust you will enjoy meeting me as I would you. You see, though I may not know you, I have prayed for you and God knows who you are. I know Him and He has told me about you. He has told me He was going to bring this book to your attention. I pray He will richly bless you as you consider its content.

There are a lot of Scripture references that go along with some of these essays. Feel free to bypass examining each one from among them. These are there so you can go as deep in your thoughts as you like with regards to what, or why I say something. Maybe here and there you will want to look a verse up to better grasp what is written. Let the Lord be your guide. If for reading me you receive anything of blessing to you, I will have achieved my goal in writing. Enough said. Adventure awaits you as you begin your, <u>A Month That Matters</u>, reading!

- L. R. Abbott

# CONTENTS

"For the LORD does not see as man sees, for man looks on the outward appearance, but the LORD looks on the heart."

People have strong inclinations to judge people by what they can see of them. I know I do. For several years my son frequented a "dojo"- a karate studio. He worked his way through skills required to earn consecutive colored belts. These belts represented increasing progress at the art of karate. The last belt to earn is the coveted black belt. Along the way my son, together with other students, received instruction, motivation and encouragement from his "sensei"- the dojo owner, teacher and expert.

Over time, as I witnessed the determination and energy students needed to increase their skills, one black belted individual especially caught my attention. Black belt level students are precise in their movements, so fluid and powerful in their leg kicks and arm thrusts, but this young man was not. He stood out as different from the rest. Though wearing a black belt, and apparently making effort to move as others, his timing was always off, his physical moves erratic, his arms and legs jerking this way and that. Only in time did my bewilderment about him became a memorable blessing.

As I frequented the dojo, I discovered this young man was a special student, an enthusiast with both mental and physical handicap. Nonetheless he was always in attendance at classes, his attitude was great, he gave an evident 100% of himself to whatever his sensai asked him to do. He was a credit to his sensai and his karate studio. In short, this young man had heart, and his sensai recognized and rewarded him for it... he got a deserved black belt.

Is that not doing things the way they should be done! It is, but it doesn't happen by looking on the outward appearance. Thankfully, that is how God judges things, by looking at our hearts. Because He does, we are rewarded at what we are handicapped at. Our actions are not always fluid in movement with what is required for reward. Our crippling by sin sees to that, yet God looks beyond our faulty actions and sees our heart.

Praise God that, despite our shortcomings, our personal sensai the Holy Spirit, our teacher and expert, helps us acquire our spiritual black belt in the dojo of God's world. Thank God too, because He knows, even if we don't... we are all His special students.

*Lord, I want to be like you.*

*Help me to not judge others by their outward appearance.*

*"Fight the good fight."*

Some stories are worth repeating. I think this is one of them. Within us all is a desire to see justice prevail, to witness good overcome evil.

During my father's training as a World War 2 soldier, he had a very difficult officiating sergeant. The man was big bodied, foulmouthed and uncouth. He was a prejudiced individual whose maltreatment of all under his charge left little reason for their respect. To make matters worse, the sergeant had singled out one soldier for especially ill treatment. That soldier was Cuban, not large in stature, enjoyed by his peers. All the same, when the sergeant made his vicious verbal attacks and demanded more unreasonable things of him than of anyone else, his fellow recruits were in no position to come to his relief.

One day, matters between the sergeant and the Cuban came to a head. After particularly intense verbal abuse toward the recruit, with distain the sergeant said, "You'd like nothing better than for me to take these stripes off so you could punch me in the face! Isn't that right?" With a reply of "Sir, yes, sir!" the die was cast. It was going to happen... the sergeant was going to give him his chance.

Although it was general knowledge the confrontation was going to take place, the location and time was not. As things would have it, my father was able to find out and, taking another man with him, one early morning the two made their way to a secluded area on the base. There, they found a place to keep out of sight and awaited the contestants' arrival. While waiting, my father thought of something he was privy to... something he was sure the sergeant was not aware of. The Cuban soldier the sergeant was about to tangle with was a Golden Gloves boxer. If nothing else, my Dad figured this match was going to be interesting.

Here is the bottom line on the fight. The Cuban tore that sergeant up. He messed him up so bad, the sergeant was unable to return to work that day and, out of necessity, was transferred never to return.

As Christians we need to be able to stand[1] up for ourselves. Trials[2] are guaranteed to be part of our lives and we are foolish and naive to imagine that foulmouthed, uncouth, prejudiced, heavy-weight accuser of our souls,[3] Satan, will not be against us. When he is, we need to find a secluded place[4] and take that destroyer[5] down. We can do it using the Word of God in spoken prayer, just as Jesus did during His own "Golden Gloves victory" over Satan in the wilderness.[6]

If we will ask the Lord to "teach our hands to war,"[7] we can all be "Golden Glove boxers,"[8] able to deliver knock out blows to the adversary of our Christian life.[9]

*Lord, teach me how to stand firm against the Devil's attacks.*
*I want to resist him so he will flee.*

1) 1 Corinthians 16:13

2) John 16:33

3) Revelation 12:10

4) Matthew 6:6

5) John 10:10

6) Matthew 4:1-11

7) 2 Samuel 22:35

8) 1 Corinthians 9:26

9) James 4:7

*"Awake, you who sleep, arise from the dead,*

*and Christ will give you light."*

"Breathe! Breathe!" the doctor commanded, as he spanked a new born baby slow to take its first breath. Only after it does are the hearts of anxious parents able to fully rejoice. Thank God, their child is out of danger. That is how the gift of physical life always works. This physical breath is God's to give[1], or to take away[2].

Artie, a 53 year old truck driver, had his breath taken away. While driving one day he had a sudden, severe heart attack and hit a utility pole. He was fortunate. The incident happened in front of a fire station. Trained individuals immediately came to his rescue. All the same, what followed did not transpire with ease. Emergency workers had to pull Artie, not a small man, out of the truck and immediately lay him on the ground. Precious minutes had passed and Artie had turned blue from lack of oxygen. The on scene portable defibrillator was used to deliver jolts of electricity to his unresponsive heart. *"BREATHE! BREATHE!"* the emergency worker ordered. Thank God, Artie's heart eventually began to beat. Later, after the crisis was over, Artie reported that the command to "Breathe! Breathe!" had registered in his ears, that this is what had given him the spark to do what he needed to do and, at that moment, what he needed to do was – *BREATHE!*

Having physical breath is a wonderful thing. With it we are able to live our lives. It is why we can enjoy picnics, movies, work, family, restaurants and more. But is having physical breath all the breath needed to live a meaningful life? No, there is another essential breath required. It is the breath of God. We do not have it when we are born. At physical birth God gives us the breath necessary for physically breathing. This enables our souls to live life in our physical body. The breath needed for spiritual breathing is another matter. God only gives this to those who are "born again."[3] Just as we cannot realize the benefits of physical life until we breathe physically, neither can we experience the benefits of spiritual life until we can breathe spiritually. This only happens when we are born again. The Greek meaning of "born again" literally means "born from above." This refers to God's accomplishing our spiritual birth when we receive his son, Jesus Christ, as our all sufficient savior. It is at that point the breath of eternal life, the Holy Spirit, takes up residence within us[4] and we begin to breathe spiritually. It is then we are able to begin to live the meaningful life that God wants for us.[5]

Have you heard it? It's the voice of the Lord. He is saying, *"BREATHE! BREATHE!"* For those who hear Him and respond by receiving His spiritual breath, new life awaits and Heaven rejoices.[6]

A chorus from an old hymn says it so well. Let it be your prayer. . .

> *Breathe on me breath of God,*
> *Fill me with life anew*

*Then I shall be what I should be*

*and do what I should do.*

1) Genesis 2:7

2) Psalm 104:29

3) John 3:3

4) John 20:22

5) John 10:10

6) Luke 15:10

*"He who does not take up his cross and follow after Me*

*is not worthy of Me."*

I drove in an unusual road race when in college. It was a competition one of my professors put together for her students. The race rewarded us for correct answers related to our studies. Getting right answers meant making progress towards the race's finish.

At the start of the race each vehicle's participants were handed a "race exam." Together they then decided the correct response to the first of a series of multiple choice questions. Alongside each possible answer were different directions, so having the right solution mattered... conclude the wrong response and time would be lost going the wrong way. On the other hand, choose correctly, and you go the right way to be rewarded with reaching a landmark. From there the next question would be discussed, the answer agreed on, and its directions pursued. This went on, so forth and so on, until the final race destination was arrived at.

So, how did it go? Not without difficulty. Some cars had less studious individuals in them... that made deriving right answers harder. Figuring out what went wrong also made for some anxious moments. Just the same, when participants saw the race's end, everyone had to agree, participating had been worth the effort. This was because the surprise finish turned out to be at the teacher's house where she was barbecuing in anticipation of her students' arrival.

When people become Christians it is not a road race they enter, but a "life race."[1] There are many questions to be considered along the way. There are twists and turns to navigate, landmarks to arrive at, as well as the need to backtrack from time to time in order to stay on course. Any anxious moments will be worth it all when the race finish is reached. Our master teacher[2] will be awaiting us in anticipation of our arrival.[3] He will not be barbecuing. Instead, He will have prepared a full banquet for us[4] and we will have arrived at our own eternal home.[5]

*Lord, help me follow your directions in my race of life.*

*I want to please you all along the way and finish well.*

1) Hebrews 12:1

2) John 3:2

3) John 17:24

4) Revelation 19:9

5) John 14:2

*"He who believes in Me, as the Scripture has said,*

*out of his heart will flow rivers of living water."*

While living in the landlocked country of Niger, West Africa, I visited the remote home of an elderly man by the name of El Qabus (pronounced Kaboose). He lived on the edge of one of the most inhospitable places on planet earth – the Sahara Desert. Looking to the horizon in every direction from his one room, stick hut, I saw nothing but a hard, uninterrupted, flat surface covered with rocks. The entire landscape varied just slightly in shades of brown because here, as elsewhere, it takes water to grow anything green.

Precious little water is readily available in this region of Africa. Wells, most often hand dug, are as close as people get to having a reliable source of precious water. Where El Qabus lives, the most water ever seen is when an uncommon rain storm leaves behind a large pool of water in a depression of earth. Imagine El Qabus's reaction when as an old man he fulfilled his lifelong desire to view something he'd previously only heard spoken of... the Niger River.

The Niger River is a wide, constantly flowing body of water that traverses through Niger. It is a home to hippos, crocodiles, fish and birds. The earth is green along its banks, making soil fertile, rich for vegetable and fruit gardens that line its sides.

During his days of Bible retreat in Niamey (Knee-am-ay), Niger's capitol, El Qabus spent all his spare time strolling beside and enjoying the greatest environmental spectacle of his life. No temporary rain pool was this! No well that might run dry! This was a seemingly endless flow of water moving at his feet. What a contrast for a man accustomed to a shortage of water! It is not surprising his longing was to observe that river as often as he could.

What that river was to El Qabus, so he was to us who knew him. How better to explain his serenity and spiritual joy than that he had a river of life flowing out of his innermost being. Just like the Niger River attracted him, so he attracted us and we wanted to be near him. After all, it was not natural that, having lived his entire life in so harsh an environment as the Sahara, he should evidence the deep sense of peace and security he credited to his relationship with Jesus Christ.[1]

El Qabus is in heaven now and he, along with all of God's children, will one day stand by another riverbank[2] where the water will be "clear as crystal, proceeding from the throne of God and the Lamb."[3] Who knows? Perhaps, even now, El Qabus is strolling its banks, reminded of an earlier pilgrimage he made to another river.

*Lord, thank you for those through who your living water flows.*
*Make me to be like them.*

1) Psalm 46:4

2) Romans 5:1

3) Revelation 22:1

*"A servant of the LORD must not quarrel but be gentle to all, able to teach, patient, in humility correcting those who are in opposition, if God perhaps will grant them repentance, so that they may know the truth"*

A Buddhist minded friend of mine gave me a chuckle when he shared with me this joke – What did the Buddhist man answer the hot dog vendor who asked him, "What do you want on it?" The Buddhist man replied, "Make me one with everything!"

As you can tell, my friend is a good natured fellow. Nonetheless, he has proved difficult to share the good news of Jesus Christ with. He is very serious about his present worldview and not easily stirred to investigate the Scriptures for himself. It is not that he does not respect Jesus as a wise teacher, or so he says but, if that were true, why wouldn't he give deeper thought to what Christ teaches?

This friend's bedroom wall has a picture of Christ hanging on it. It has a prominent place right next to images of Buddha, Krishna and other Buddhist deities. Sadly, to him Jesus was not the sinless Son of God in human flesh, the only one who lived a sinless life and died a substitutionary death for the sins of others. It follows in natural consequence then that he would not believe in a risen, ascended savior who is sitting at God's right hand. No, this man is presently, "in the dark"[1], yet to have the "light of life"[2] dawn upon him.

What can I do for my friend? What can you do for yours of similar need? Pray... love... be patient, be prepared to share out of your care, then pray some more. Over time such things can make a way to their heart where there presently appears to be none.

I remember as a young man learning of Mr. LeTourneau, a Christian engineer of selfless financial giving and many inventions to his name. One machine he designed was gigantic in size and nothing less than fantastic in what it could do. It can chew through a forest in front of it and leave a completed road ready to ride behind it! It is not a fast machine, but it *is* effective.

LeTourneau's machine is similar to how our Christian witness often works, not necessarily fast, but it gets the job done. When the way our witness prepares is complete... then there is a way, a way through the forest of obstacles that previously hindered the gospel's advance.

Let's be persistent in our witness, because our witness does work.


*Lord, lead me to people who you have prepared to receive my witness. Move them out of darkness and into your light.*


1) Ephesians 4:18

2) John 8:12

**Preachers**

*"So then faith comes by hearing,*

*and hearing by the word of God."*

Has your experience listening to preachers been like mine, some are easy to listen to, others more difficult? Some articulate their words... that makes them easy to understand. I like that. Others are more monotone in speech, never varying in volume or expression. That makes me sleepy. Some are the opposite, raising and lowering their voice for effect at appropriate moments. That works for me. It helps keep me awake. There is one preaching style that gives me a tough time - "the yeller." You know, the preacher whose volume is set on high for protracted periods of time. Personally, I do not enjoy that, but I know there are people who feel they have not heard preaching unless the presenter works up a sweat, gets a little red in the face and often declares something like, "Oh, thank you Holy Ghost." This usually happens at times which coincide with the speaker's own personal enlightenment received at the podium. Those preachers always come with a hanky to wipe the sweat from their foreheads. There are also the "gulpers," the messengers whose speed of delivery seems to demand they take in large measures of air. This is often accompanied by a guttural sound that accentuates the fact the speaker is on a roll and probably not about to stop anytime soon.

Now, if you have gone to the same church all your life, if you've not been one to get around much in the wide, wide, world of

Christendom, you will less likely identify with all I just described. It is very possible you have listened to your one, same pastor, or people like him, for the last thirty years. There is nothing wrong with that if you are being fed well. *That*, more than anything else, is what is important when it comes to preachers... content, content, content. What is he saying? Is it Scriptural? Does it encourage, build up, teach of God, His ways and purposes? As listeners, our ears are to be open to what is said and how it applies to us. When we have the choice, we will naturally gravitate towards preaching that provides the content we need and presented in the style we enjoy.

Brother, sister, if you have occasion to find yourself listening to the delivery of God's Word in a manner not all to your pleasure, try not to be judgmental. There are regional, cultural, educational, denominational, and preacher personal reasons which make for different styles used in the presentation of God's Word. Make an effort to get past what bugs you in any of God's messengers you hear. Do not be taken off target. Ask yourself, "What is the man saying?" Or, better yet, ask "What might God want to say to me through this man?" Listen for the preacher's heartbeat. Hear it and be blessed!

*Lord, when your Word is preached help me to hear it.*
*Bless all your messengers and make them fruitful.*

*"By Him all things were created that are in heaven*
*and that are on earth."*

I was thumbing through a magazine when a singular, black and white photograph arrested my attention. Within it appeared a small office where a desk was paired with an empty, well-worn leather back chair. Behind these were two wall shelves stocked with books and, between these two shelves stretched a chalkboard filled with mysterious mathematical equations. As I read, I learned the photo was taken on April 18, 1955, just hours after the man who had previously occupied the office had died. His name – none other than the world renowned physicist, Albert Einstein. What was the professor last working on before death took him? A clue was found atop his desk... unfinished notes on what he had entitled, "A Theory of Everything."

I imagine most people would consider impossible an all-encompassing theory that could explain everything. After all, it does seem a rather large subject! Nonetheless, the thought was not absurd to the highly intelligent man who discovered the formula for the atomic bomb and neither should it be for the believer of the Bible. Those who are familiar with the teachings of God's Word are aware everything was created by God for His glory.[1] They know too that, under girding all things, God has orderly, consistent scientific laws which have been progressively discovered by man.

I am not sure what direction Mr. Einstein was going in his unfinished work, but one thing is certain... had he lived longer, whatever discovery he might have arrived at would have had to point to a creator.[2]  This is because, from the smallest thing seen through a microscope, to the largest thing seen in a telescope, along with everything seen in between and unseen beyond, *everything* points to the design of an infinitely intelligent and almighty God.[3]

*Lord, help me to see your wisdom and design in everything.*

1) Psalm 19:1

2) John 1:3

3) Proverbs 30:4

**The "*WOW!*" Factor** *Ps. 119:130*

*"The entrance of Your words gives light;*

*It gives understanding to the simple."*

The other day I was visiting with a friend who has great difficulty to read. In hand I took a copy of the Good News version of the Gospel of John.

To appreciate what was about to happen, you need to know, this 47 year old friend grew up in a church experience which extolled the virtues of the King James version of the Bible and used it only. As a result, what with his own reading challenge and all, he had not spent the time in God's Word which would have been helpful in provoking his spiritual growth. Previous to this present visit with him, I had suggested he consider adopting a simpler to read version of the Word of God to read, but I was rebuffed for even suggesting the idea. Now, here he was with this paraphrased Gospel of John in his hands.

"Why don't you sit down and read for us a bit," I suggested. He demurred at first, uncertain of his own ability to pronounce the many "big words" he expected to encounter. "It's ok," I encouraged, "I will help you as needed." That was all it took and he was off and reading. For the next two hours! Yes, sometimes he faltered at various words, some were challenging to him. I said, "You're not the only one who finds some of these challenging!" Here though is what blessed me above all else... frequently, throughout his reading, he would pause, appear to me to ponder in silence, then enthusiastically express himself by proclaiming, "*Wow!*"[1] This happened repeatedly. Eventually, I realized, more was going on here than just a man feeling he was reading his Bible well for the first time. Evidently, he was understanding it too, receiving its life giving light.[2]

As my friend's reading went on, and his "*Wows!*" went along with it, I began to feel as though I was missing out on something. However, that changed when I paid less attention on the accuracy of his reading and more attention to what the Scriptures were saying. Then his "*Wow!*" became my "*Wow!*" What a blessing![3]

*Lord, help me keep the wonder*

*in my reading of your Word.*

1) Psalm 119:161b

2) Psalm 18:28

3) Psalm 119:103

**<u>Surprise Guest</u>**

*"For this purpose the Son of God was manifested,*

*that He might destroy the works of the devil."*

One bad weather night while living in Nigeria, West Africa, my wife and I entertained a surprise guest. Here is how it happened...

Knowing from previous experience that wind had the potential to push rainwater under the front door of our home, we stuffed a towel under the bottom of the door before going to bed. Deciding to see if it had worked to discourage the problem, I rose from bed during the night, picked up my flashlight and headed for the living room. Imagine my surprise when the glow of my light fell upon a 2 ½ foot snake sleeping on top of that towel! Now, I appreciate creatures of all sorts but, in a situation like that, when I did not know if the snake was venomous, I'm going to follow the rule of thumb known around the world, "the only good snake is a dead snake." The only question was, how to do the deed? Realizing I needed an extra hand, I awoke my wife so she could hold the light on our guest. Me, I had my trusty "lunga-lunga" in hand – what amounts to being an African machete. With it, like David against Goliath, I lifted that lunga-lunga and brought it down with a thud, cleanly severing the giant's head from its body. I'm sure I remember my wife's voice say, "My hero!" Or not... perhaps she just turned and went back to bed, but I like to think it happened that way.

Something worthy of mention happened the day after our surprise guest parted (pun intended). Some African friends had heard of our encounter and wanted to see what remained of the snake. What they saw confirmed their concern – the snake was of the sort which has the ability to spit a debilitating liquid at an aggressor... and they always shoot for the eyes. They warned us the way I had dispatched our night visitor had been dangerous. Often, the severed head of this kind of snake retains some moments of life in which it is known to possibly still spit. This is why Africans who know better always crush this snake's head instead of cutting it off.

Another thing. Our friends wanted us to know there is a remedy for the unfortunate person who has this snake spit in their eyes. It is this... wash the eyes out with milk. Milk neutralizes the acidic nature of the serpent's venom.

This incident made me wonder. Was Satan this variety of snake? After all, he loves to operate in the dark,[1] and he spits in peoples' eyes, blinding their minds[2] to Christ's deity and redemptive work. Thankfully, God has provided the "milk"[3] of his Word as remedy to the acidic nature of the Devil's toxin.[4] What's more, God's Son, crushed[5] that 'ol serpent's[6] head at Calvary.[7] Makes you wonder, doesn't it?

*Lord, thank you for your victory over Satan.*

*Help me to not fall for his lies and deception.*

*I want clear vision of you.*

1) Ephesians 6:12

2) 2 Corinthians 4:4

3) 1 Peter 2:2

4) John 8:44

5) Genesis 3:15

6) Revelation 20:2

7) Luke 24:6, 7

**<u>Healthy Hearts</u>**

*"I will give you a new heart*

*and put a new spirit within you."*

The work of a deceased cardiologist and his grandson is saving lives today. The doctor had a 50 year career during which he recorded 125 irregular heartbeats on compact discs. When his grandson found these when exploring his grandfather's belongings, he put together a computer code and application to make them useful. Using their cell phone with what he has done, people can compare their own heartbeat against those which are irregular. Since this has been available, numerous people have benefited, but none of closer relationship to the grandson then his own mother. She, a doctor herself, was forewarned of a problem by her son's program just several months before having open-heart surgery that saved her life.

There is another son who saved his mother's life in similar manner. As consequence of the fall, Mary, the mother of Jesus, was born with the same irregular heartbeat that affects us all. Listened to through a stethoscope it would sound like, "me-me, me-me, me-me." However, at some time Mary had obviously compared her own irregular spiritual heartbeat against the right one found in God's Word. When Mary testified saying, "My soul magnifies the Lord and my spirit rejoices in God my Savior,"[1] she spoke to the fact she had previously submitted to God's spiritual heart surgery.

How about you?  Have you received the spiritual heart surgery God wants for you?[2] If we were able to listen to your spiritual heartbeat, what would it sound like?  Would it be heard to beat, "me - me, me - me, me - me?"  Or, would it sound like Mary's, whose heart repeated, "God - God, God - God, God - God?"[3]

*Lord, give me a selfless heart that beats for you.*

1) Luke 1:46, 47; 6:45

2) Romans 2:29; 2 Corinthians 13:5

3) Mark 12:30

*"If anyone adds to these things, God will add to him the plagues that are written in this book; and if anyone takes away from the words of the book of this prophecy, God shall take away his part from the Book of Life."*

There is an error many people make. They speak of "the Book of Revelations" and refer to the "fruits of the Spirit." Did you catch the error? What ought to be said is, "the Book of Revelation" and "the fruit of the Spirit." By now you have probably caught on to what I am getting at. It is not accurate to pluralize the words "Revelation" or "fruit" in these cases. These are easy errors to make and not of any dire consequence. That said, there are some serious errors that can be made in the use of Scriptures and they matter greatly. They should be avoided. One of them is to add something to the truth of God's Word that is not there. Another is to subtract something from the God's truth that is there. To do either is to invite error and it is this sort of thing false prophets and false teachers do.[1] Admittedly, some of Scripture is not easy to understand, but this does not give anyone license to twist Scripture to mean something quite different from what God intends.[2] Accurate use of the Scriptures is a matter of life or death, so there should be no adding or subtracting.

No adding to or subtracting from the Bible... I get that. But is there something we can do with it? Yes, we can divide what God has given. He wants us to. He says, "Study to show yourself approved, a workman that does not need to be ashamed, rightly *dividing* the Word of truth."[3] This should be encouraging to us - well, it is for me anyway. You see, for me, math was my weakest subject in school. But, in God's math class, we only have to master division! So, if we are looking for answers, seeking truth, trying to find out God's will and ways, or searching for a vision, let's do it by comparing Scripture with Scripture. As is said in 1 Corinthians 2:1, God will teach us, "not with the words which man's wisdom teaches, but which the Holy Spirit teaches; comparing spiritual things with spiritual."

All the spiritual understanding we need is found in the Bible.[4] Do you need to brush up on your division skills?

*Holy Spirit, please help me to compare*
*and divide God's Word accurately.*

1)  2 Peter 2:1

2)  2 Peter 3:16

3)  2 Timothy 2:15

4)  2 Timothy 3:16, 17

*"I will be a Father to you, and you shall be My sons and daughters, says the LORD Almighty."*

I viewed a report about a morbidly obese 28 year old who was living at home with his parents. Get this - his mother still powders him after his bath, cooks for him, does his laundry, etc. etc. He does not work and he owes his parents a lot of money. The majority of his days are spent in his bedroom eating snack food and playing games. What's wrong with this picture? What's not! The parents are enabling their child to be ill-equipped for life. Their approach to parenting their son is doing him no favors. If anything, it is crippling him from experiencing essential personal growth.

What needs to be done? They need to get him out on his own. Now, it may surprise you to hear this, but he wants to be on his own. What prevents him? For one, human nature being what it is, home is all he has known. All of his needs have been met within the same walls for a very long time. This just naturally means there is a great lack of incentive to move out on his part. There's another thing. His mother is unable to "cut the apron string" to him. She dotes and worries over him and what he would do in the "real world."

There is no doubt in my mind, the parents in this sad scenario are contributing to, and are in large part responsible for, the situation in which their son finds himself. The young man needs to be put out on his own if he is ever to realize his full potential. Unfortunately, in our deteriorating culture, in varying forms, scenarios like this are occurring more often than we might like to believe.

As a Christ follower, I am thrilled that I have a heavenly father who knows exactly how to parent me. In no way does He disable me by enabling me to live in an unhealthy manner. He knows when and how to discipline me and does it. As I respond to His chastening,[1] He keeps me rightly related to life and walking in step with Him. I appreciate that He "lets me go," but He also goes with me.[2]

No earthly parents are perfect in their parenting, but how wonderful to have a heavenly father who is.[3]

*Lord, thank you for always doing what is best for me.*

1) Hebrews 12:9-11

2) Matthew 28:20b

3) Psalm 18:30a

*"The days are coming," says the Lord GOD, "That I will send a famine on the land, not a famine of bread, nor a thirst for water, but of hearing the words of the Lord."*

Cassava (the "c" is pronounced like a "k" and all short vowels) is a West African staple food that grows in the ground much like a potato, but it is not so nutritious as many other plants that are grown that way. As a matter of fact, cassava is a quite non-nutritious food source. "Whoa," you say, "a non-nutritious staple food?" Raises alarm bells doesn't it? Here is what is behind that... It is not that it is wonderfully tasty, many people would prefer to eat something else. Its big attraction is that it grows easily in arid places where there is little water. This is the geographical situation for many in the Sahara region of Africa. For many, little water is the norm. Hence, because cassava grows easily, there is plenty of it and it is not costly. Are you getting the picture? Cassava is readily available and is inexpensive. In a land of great poverty, where there are recurring famines, it is no surprise then that its use is actually a recipe for physical disaster. Cassava can fill the peoples' stomachs, but it will not deliver the nutrients required for healthy living. Because of a poorly balanced diet, people can only exist on it for so long before malnutrition sets in.

This world's human population is in a state of spiritual famine. They are spiritually malnourished for lack of digesting the Word of

God.[1] If we viewed them spiritually, we would see them with distended bellies, glazed eyes and parched, cracked lips. They are feeding on the "cassava" of the world. They are full, but not of what satisfies, not of what nourishes the souls.[2] The one "agricultural product" that can satisfy them is the manna God makes available in Christ.[3]

This life presents itself as a challenge to all of us.[4] But, like the Israelites who consumed manna in the wilderness for 40 years,[5] we who walk with the Lord are sustained by our daily intake of God's Word.[6] We sow and cultivate this manna in our hearts so we can reap the healthy benefits it provides.[7]

Keeping in mind what has been said about cassava, let's return to West Africa for a moment. I have some good news. There are Christian mission agencies and aid groups who have been introducing new, more nutritious food sources to substitute for this non-nutritious plant. Does that give you an idea as to what you and I can do to improve the spiritual diet of others in our sphere of influence? Right! We can introduce them to the manna, to the Word of God. As someone once said, "Evangelism is just one beggar telling another beggar where to find bread."

The bread of God's Word is a wholesome food source... the things of this world are not. Let's purpose to share our manna liberally.

*Lord, guide me in pointing people to your wonderful Word.*

1) Matthew 4:4

2) Romans 3:10-18

3) John 6:51

4) Isaiah 14:16, 17

5) Acts 13:18

6) Psalm 81:10

7) Matthew 13:18-23

*"Go out into the highways and hedges,*
*and compel them to come in, that my house may be filled."*

You never know what will happen when you reach out to someone in Jesus' name. Whether you accept the challenge to walk across a room to introduce yourself to a stranger, go door to door to invite people to church, or travel overseas to build cross-cultural relationships, there is no way of knowing what God will do.[1]

A partner and I were volunteers in a church's door to door outreach. Once a week for three weeks we visited the same homes with gospel literature and an invitation to church. Most contacts were satisfied to meet us at their door, but knocking at one stranger's door resulted in an invitation to come inside. The home owner, Reggie, was excited to see us. He said he had heard we were moving through the community and he wondered when we would be getting around to him. We noticed that spread out on his coffee table were books on the supernatural, along with materials on UFOs and religion. The many religious themed pictures on his living room walls also caught our attention.

As Reggie explained it, he was of a Catholic background, yet still searching for something he had not found. Apparently he was interested to show us his depth of sincerity, because he invited us to see his "shrine of worship." It turned out to be on top of his chest of drawers in his bedroom. There, neatly arranged, was a standing cross, a picture of Mary, another of Jesus, and some candles. It was here that he said he came to pray each day.

After returning to Reggie's living room, we shared the gospel with him. He listened with rapt attention to our every word. On conclusion, he commented that it was all very interesting, that he would certainly give it some thought and read our literature. The next thing we knew, Reggie became a regular attender at church, got saved and was baptized.

Only three months after first meeting Reggie, the telephone rang. The voice on the other end of the line said, "Reggie was at his doctor's office this morning for a scheduled appointment when he collapsed and died." Our church's dear, dear, brother was gone.

Reggie's wife, from whom he had been separated, was at his funeral service. She asked me the question, "Why was my husband such a different man in the last three months of his life? What a delight for her to receive both the answer to her question,[2] as well as the Savior who made Reggie's wonderful testimony possible.[3]

The next time you have an opportunity to reach out to someone in Jesus' name – do it. You never know what will happen when you do.[4]

*Lord, help me take advantage of opportunities*

*to share you with others.*

1) Ephesians 3:20

2) 2 Corinthians 5:17

3) Revelation 3:20

4) Acts 3:6-8

*"The works of the flesh are evident... But the fruit of the Spirit is love, joy, peace, longsuffering, kindness, goodness, faithfulness, gentleness, self-control."*

The year was 1969. I was excited about a Ford Mustang, my first car. This was despite the fact my friends poked fun at my choice of car. Why would they do that? They did it because they were all Chevy enthusiasts. Nevertheless, that car served me well as my daily ride for the next ten years, a fact not lost on my good natured, Chevy loving buddies. Eventually they had to concede that, while their own choices in transportation had come and gone, mine still remained.

No matter if your choice is a Cadillac, Ford, Chevy, VW or some other model, any one of them in good operating condition could get you where you want to go. Not so for the many things you may permit to drive you.[1] If anger, lust, jealousy, selfish ambition or the like are a driving force in your life, they will assuredly take you to places you do not want to arrive.[2]

It is good to give consideration to what you will drive, but it is more important you let yourself be driven only by those actions which will help you avoid wrecking on the road of life.[3] I suggest a vehicle inspection of your own soul.[4] Ask yourself, "What is driving me at this time?" Answer this and you will have insight about where you can expect to arrive.[5] Next, ask yourself, "Is that really where I want to go?" Then, if you are heading where you do not wish to arrive,[6] change drivers.[7] When you do, make sure that what you permit to drive you is legal in the eyes of the Lord.[8] Honesty, love, patience and self-control, are among some of His own choices[9] to be your daily drivers. They will take you to where you will be happy to arrive.[10]

*Lord, help me be habitually controlled by actions and attitudes you can approve of.*

1) Romans 8:7

2) Romans 8:13a

3) Romans 8:13b

4) 1 Corinthians 11:28a

5) Matthew 7:13, 14

6) Galatians 5:19-21

7) Romans 12:1, 2

8) Psalm 119:1-7

9) Galatians 5:22-25

10) Revelation 3:12

*"Whatever things are noble... are just... are pure... are lovely...
are of good report, if there is any virtue and if there is anything
praiseworthy - meditate on these things."*

Thinking is a necessary but seemingly nebulous activity. We tend to take it for granted because we have done so much of it. For the most part it goes unnoticed by us. Often we wrongly regard it as background activity to what we do. Yet it is not secondary to our actions, but primary to and preceding them. Did you pick up a fork, comb your hair, or open your mouth to speak? You did not unless the thought to do so came before your action. The same can be said about a person lying, stealing, getting angry, losing control, or a host of other damaging practices. Such is what makes this subject of thought so great in importance. Awesome things our minds! Not at all unlike a sophisticated computer.

I remember when I learned my computer had a "sleep mode." I chuckled to hear it. I said, "My computer wants to go to sleep?" Setting aside the "wants to," I did learn that my computer does "sleep"... that at my command it powers down to save energy while not in use. This is done in lieu of turning it completely off. To me, what is interesting about this is that in sleep mode the computer is still running. Our minds operate in the same way. We power them down to rest while we sleep but, like the computer, our minds are not turned off – they are just "powered down." No doubt this has much to do with the production of dreams.

So it is that, whether awake or asleep, our thought life is one of ceaseless activity. This is why it is important we not disassociate ourselves from what is taking place in our minds. To do so is to invite loss of control over our actions and this is the reason for so much woe in the world. Too many people do not allow for God and His Word to have control over what they are thinking.

Remember this, the Bible is the only "self-help" book that will make your mind what it needs to be and take you where you want to go. Its influence will help you think correctly and right actions will naturally follow. Here then is the bottom line – when you think right you will act appropriately, and the world, your world, will be a better place. Your thoughts *do* matter!

*Lord, help me think in ways that please you and will not be detrimental to myself or others.*

1) Peter 1:13-15

*"You know how to discern the face of the sky,*
*but you cannot discern the signs of the times."*

I loved to go salt water fishing with my father when I was a kid. He taught me how to bait my hook, catch and clean fish, as well as watch the weather.   He said watching the weather was very important, that inattention to doing so was an invitation to be caught in rough seas and dangerous circumstances. "Never forget Bob," he would say, "Red sky in the morning means sailor take warning!"  I never forgot it – a red sky in the morning is often the precursor to a foul weather day.

Much as fishermen study the sky in order to make plans and stay safe, our heavenly father wants us to understand the times we live in.  While some people dare God to strike them with lightning, and others seem to want God to fall out of the sky before they will acknowledge his existence, the evidence of the near hour when God will show his wrath continues its approach.  The deteriorating state of cultures, societies, families and people on earth screams out what the Bible says to expect, that things will get worse, not better in the world.  This is contrary to what many people imagine is a right Biblical view.  They have a "pie in the sky" sort of attitude that somehow, someway, mans' "goodness" is going to deliver the world to a better future, as if God plays "nicey, nicey" as regards their rebellion.  He does not.  It's just not Scriptural to think so.

Sin is the problem and being nice towards sin is not consistent with who the holy God is. The truth is that *there will be* those people who are the objects of His wrath.[1] 2 Timothy 3:13 says, "In the last days, evil men will grow worse and worse." This is because man is innately evil, not good.[2] 2 Timothy 3:2-5 says, "Men will be lovers of themselves, lovers of money, boasters, proud, blasphemers, disobedient to parents, unthankful, unholy, unloving, unforgiving, slanders, without self-control, brutal, despisers of good, traitors, headstrong, haughty, lovers of pleasure rather than lovers of God, having a form of godliness but denying its power." Such are the recognizable signs of our times and they do not point to things improving.

The morning skies are red around the world today. If people refuse to see it, they are like a fisherman who ignores obvious signs of warning. By so doing, he puts his and his crews' lives in danger. How much better to be wise, read the signs of our times, and be in safe harbor when the storm hits.[3]

*Lord, thank you that your Son is a refuge of safety from your wrath.*

1) Hebrews 3:11, 12

2) Mark 13:33-37

3) Romans 3:10-18

**<u>Passionate People</u>**

*"To you it has been granted on behalf of Christ, not only to believe in Him, but also to suffer for His sake."*

Thank God for passionate people! Without them where would this world be? A good person's passionate emotion lets nothing prevent them from expending the energy and sacrifice necessary to make progress towards the accomplishment of some worthy goal. The passionate person is not deterred by difficulties and obstacles. Their eye is on the prize, the achieving of something valued and worth fighting for. Passionate people ought to be supported, appreciated and emulated by other good people so far as their own enthusiasm for the task can be mustered. Yet often, the most passionate among us must work against the tide of others who do not share their worthy burden. Such a one was William Wiberforce.

Englishman William Wilberforce became a Christian in 1784, a time when the British economy was undergirded by the forced slavery of black people. The passion of Wilberforce against the inhuman treatment of slaves was his motive to become a member of the British parliament. Once in, he immediately sounded his call to end slavery. Over and over he gave impassioned arguments before legislators who looked down on him and thought him a fool. Nevertheless, he did not relent in letting his voice be heard in the parliamentary chamber. Sometimes he would even hold up slave chains to punctuate his message of slavery's cruelty. For years he was mocked, until finally in 1807. That was when his passion beat the overwhelming odds and laws were enacted to end the purchase and selling of any new slaves. A victory to be sure! But not enough to prevent Wilberforce's passion from carrying him forward to see existing slaves freed. He worked tirelessly for this until their freedom became reality in 1833. The document for their liberation was signed, slavery in England was abolished and, just three days after, William Wilberforce died.

Would it surprise you if I said I think I have seen Mr. Wilberforce recently in my own metropolitan area? In actual fact, I do not know the man's name, but I think Mr. Wilberforce would not mind my using his. The reason is, I saw passion at work in this person, someone more concerned with the truth of an injustice he wanted reformed than how foolish he may look to others. He did not brandish chains. Instead, he displayed baby dolls, lots of them. He wore a necklace of them, carried one in his arms and pushed another in a stroller. He had with him a sign that said, "Stop abortion NOW!" Over the years I saw him numerous times and in many different places, often in front of our state house or at any one of a number of busy intersections. He was always waving to passersby and I know he had appropriate Christian tracts he passed out. I even saw him in rain gear, undeterred by bad weather. What makes a man do that sort of thing? Passion – that's what! Yes, passion... it's something we would all do well to have more of.[1]

*Lord, I pray my heart may be moved by the things that move your heart.*

1) Colossians 3:23; Titus 2:13,14

*"The word of God is living and powerful."*

Outside is darkness, thunder and lightning flashing. Inside, a mad scientist stands with anticipation over his pieced together creation. Suddenly, a great ear piercing crackle of lightning strikes a rod atop his castle. It travels down wires that lead to an apparatus which begins to transfer power to a lifeless body spread out on top a table. As the scientist fixes his eyes intently upon what he has made, he thinks he notices a near imperceptible twitch of a finger, then - a sure jerk of a hand, after which the now life infused body begins to sit up. Amid repeating, loud claps of thunder, flashes of lightning and electrical sparks, the craze intoned voice of the creature's creator is heard to exclaim, *"It's alive! It's alive!"* So begins the tale of Mary Shelley's classic novel, Frankenstein.

Would you think it humorous if I told you I sometimes look at the Bible and say in that same craze intoned voice as the scientist, *"It's alive! It's alive!"* Why do I do that? Thank you for asking. I do it because I know the Bible is infused with the power of God. It enables us to see sin and unbelief in our own hearts. Mixed with faith, it empowers us to obey God and claim His promises. Viewing life through its pages we can actually see God and understand how He looks at us. Perhaps most amazing, the Word of God equips us to see ourselves as we really are, not just as we think ourselves to be in our own imagination.[1]

Oh, the Bible is alive alright! It is animating previously dead people[2] to do the things they could not, would not otherwise do for the glory of God.

Come on, look at your Bible and say it with me. Use the mad scientist's crazed voice if you like. Go ahead, say it... *"It's alive! It's alive!"*

*Lord, thank you for your powerful Word. Thank you that it is working in me.*

1)  2 Corinthians 10:3-5

2)  Ephesians 2:1

*"Those who wait on the LORD shall renew their strength; they shall mount up with wings like eagles, they shall run and not be weary, they shall walk and not faint."*

Before we could see who was doing it we heard singing. The voices increased in volume as we stepped outside into the brilliant African sunlight. There, in front of the home we were just settling into, was an ebullient, dancing, continuously circling group of women whose arrival had not been anticipated. The many colors and patterns of cloth they wore was an eye-catching contrast to a backdrop of parched earth and rain starved elephant grass. Initially we were puzzled. What was this about? Where did all these women come from? An English speaking student came along and explained, these were members of the local "Zuma Tomata," the ladies fellowship of an evangelical church we had come to work with. They were welcoming us to their community. A look of pure joy moved from the ladies faces to our own as we understood what this was all about. How could it have been otherwise! There they were, arms pumping this way and that, torsos bending up and down, their heads jutting in and out – and their singing! The chorus of one song seemed to summarize the reason for their enthusiasm. They were singing "ba gajiya!" Each time they sang it, their dance circle froze momentarily, all sound and movement stopped, then, just as suddenly, they erupted into more motion and song. They did this over and over again.

These ladies unstoppable zeal was the message of their song.

When they sang "ba gajiya," they were saying they had "no tiredness," no fatigue in their service[1] to Jehovah Jirah, their God who provides.[2]  They saw in us an answer to their prayers, and this was how they gave God glory, thanks and praise.[3]

If anyone had a reason to be tired, it was these women.  We marveled, knowing they had trekked in the hot sun from the other side of the Niger River, a distance of not less than four miles.

When their time with us came to an end, we readied cool water to quench our guests thirst.  Afterwards, I offered them rides home which they gratefully declined.  They said they preferred to walk home.[4]

*Lord, please help me to be energetic in my service for you.*

1) 2 Thessalonians 3:13

2) Philippians 4:19

3) 2 Samuel 6:14

4) Isaiah 40:29-31

*"We know that we are of God, and the whole world lies under the sway of the wicked one."*

America's winter of 2014 repeatedly hit with historically record breaking cold, snow and ice storms.  In many regions life seemed to come to a standstill because of impassable roads, downed trees and power outages.  For the first time weather analysts on television and radio introduced the term "arctic blast" to their vocabulary.  The new terminology describes the infusion into North America of cold temperatures normally reserved for the Polar Regions.

In the midst of 2014 winter difficulties, the one main stress reducing and problem relieving thing that soothed the seasonal difficulties was the availability of salt.  More than any other one thing, it was salt which kept America's people able to be productive.  This was because salt enabled services and goods to travel over roads otherwise impassable if not for salt's application.  Because of the great demand for it, one salt provider for a twelve state area had to increase production at its mining facility by going to three shifts and laboring 24 hours a day seven days a week.  It is likely they were the ones happiest for the severe winter since it meant more money in their pockets.

After the harsh winter of 2014 finally ended, so did the demand for road salt.  The aforementioned mining site got a much needed rest.  Their employees caught their breath, then adjusted their schedules to set an easier pace and stockpile their product for the next winter season.

The Lord knows the earth is presently in a dark time of winter,[1] so He has provided his "Salt" to deal with it.[2] His people are the salt He dispenses along the pathways of life. He does it to break up the ice of hard hearts, melt the snows of peoples' tough times, and warm those who are cold towards Him.[3] The time of demand for spiritual salt, unlike the on again, off again winter seasons of North America, is 365 days a year in every world region. This requires the Lord mine for souls[4] 24/7 in order to meet the demand for the fresh salt necessary to insure his gospel gets to where people need to hear it.[5] He is successfully accomplishing this through his crew of workers whose time to rest will come, but is not yet. Are you one of them?[6]

*Lord, help me apply myself to meeting others needs and sharing the gospel with them.*

1) 1 John 2:17

2) Matthew 5:13a

3) Isaiah 9:2

4) 2 Chronicles 16:9a

5) Acts 1:8

6) Matthew 5:13

*"...nor give place to the devil."*

Would you be surprised to be riding down the road and see an open jeep with a lion cub sitting up in the back seat? I was. Though I was in West Africa, this was still a peculiar sight. Not only that, but later the same day, I saw a different lion cub staring out a van window. What was going on? I didn't know, but soon learned these animals were the talk of the town, that there were actually four cubs in all. It turned out they had been born to a lioness at the Niamey, Niger zoo. Since the zoo had limited resources, it had assigned the cubs early care to four volunteer families who would keep them at home and feed them at their own expense. At an agreed upon time, before the cubs became dangerous, they would be returned to the zoo. We eventually took our children to one of the homes for a photo shoot. The picture turned out great... three young people gathered close to a very cooperative, big pawed, golden haired lion cub.

The temporary adoption of the four cubs was a success, except for one thing. It happened with the family we visited. They had gone on a vacation and left the care of their home and pets to a housekeeper. As was the daily habit there, one day the housekeeper put the pet gerbil inside its clear exercise sphere. This is something that, when a creature inside it walks or runs, the sphere moves around on the floor. This is not usually a problem, but this day it was. It caught the interest of the lion cub. With one bat of its paw the hatch of the sphere opened, the gerbil was thrown out and, with blazing speed, the cub gulped down a quick snack. An aghast, wide-eyed housekeeper, said it all happened so fast there was nothing she could do to prevent it.

So, like I was saying, the temporary adoption of four lion cubs was a success, unless, of course, you look at it from the perspective of one little, unfortunate gerbil. I mean, look where having a lion cub in the house got him!

1 Peter 5:8 says, "The devil walks about like a roaring lion, seeking whom he may devour." Now, I grant you, the cub couldn't roar, not yet. But he sure showed he could devour!

Is there a moral to this lion's tale? Yes, there is... The safest way to avoid the gerbil's misfortune is to not give place (opportunity) to the lion.

*Lord, help me stay clear of the devil. I do not want to give him opportunity to devour me.*

# The Restorer

*"He who has begun a good work in you will*
*complete it until the day of Jesus Christ."*


Pulling up to a gas pump one day, I found myself enamored with a nearby antique car. It was beautiful! I just had to go ask a couple of questions of what turned out to be a very happy owner. He was proud of his ride, said he had found it all weathered and rusted, hidden away in some overgrown South Carolina woods. From the vehicle's trunk he took a photo album in which were pictures from every stage of the car's restoration, part of which was sandblasting and painting. It was obvious the entire remake took a long time of enduring effort on his part.

What was it that kept this man so attentive to this demanding project? I think it was the vision he had of restoring an otherwise worthless scrap of metal to its original condition. He was able to envision what it would be like on completion, and he knew it would be worth his effort and sacrifice. The pleasure he took in the fruit of his labor was obvious and understandable.

Amid the entanglement of the woods of this world, God finds us in various stages of disuse and need of restoring. Thankfully, He goes to work on us, putting us through various situations of life that sandblast away waste and prepare us for the finished look He desires. Our restoration takes much time and effort on His part, but He is more than ready and equipped for the task.[1] His patience and commitment insure He will see us into the condition He envisions.[2] When His work is completed we are His reward, living trophies, testimonies[3] to His love and zeal[4] to accomplish what pleases Him. As beneficiaries of this divine restoration, we should often tell Him how grateful we are for His dedication and how happy we are for His success.[5]

*Lord, I praise you that you will complete the good work you have begun in me.*

1) Philippians 1:6

2) 1 John 3:2

3) 1 Peter 2:9

4) Isaiah 37:32b

5) Revelation 4:11

**<u>Can You See It?</u>**

*"And he looked up and said, I see men like trees, walking."*

"You can't see *that*?" It was a question exclaimed by my incredulous father. As he said it, he sprang out of his chair at the optometrist's office. Then, going to the other side of the room, he pointed at the largest letter on an eye chart and exclaimed again, "You can't see *this*?" No, I couldn't. I was in third grade at the time and the teacher felt I was having trouble seeing the chalkboard. So far as my father was concerned, the confirmation was now in – his son couldn't even see the largest letter on the eye chart!

There are many people with eyesight worse than mine. One of them was a blind man. An eye chart in front of him would have been of no assistance, but Jesus in front of him was. After the Savior's first touch, the man's sight became much like mine in the optometrist's office, except that, instead of seeing a blurred letter, he saw blurred people. He said, "I see men like trees, walking." However, following Jesus' second touch, "he was restored and saw everyone clearly." Thankfully, with corrective glasses, so did I.

Unlike my father's reaction at the doctor's office, the heavenly Father is not surprised at the vision impairment of the unsaved. He knows that, due to the fall,[1] all of earth's population naturally suffers from spiritual blindness. Because of the resulting darkness of this condition,[2] God has given the people of the world[3] "the light of the world,"[4] Jesus.  Touched by Him, we have through Him the corrective lens required to view accurately the eye chart of God's creation.[5]

*Lord, touch me that I may view clearly all things through your viewpoint.*

1) Genesis 3:1-6

2) Isaiah 9:2

3) John 3:16

4) John 8:12

5) 2 Corinthians 4:6

*"He who is greedy for gain troubles his own house,*
*but he who hates bribes will live."*

I'd often driven for shipment loads of airfreight into this West African airport, but never before had I seen someone stopping vehicles along the terminal's entrance road. Yet there he was, a soldier in khaki uniform with a rifle slung over his shoulder. Motioning me to pull over, he came to the driver side window saying I would need to pay him something to get into the airport. I replied that for me to do that he would have to give me a proper receipt. He said he had none and if I would not give him payment, I could just remain there by the roadside. In light of this stalemate, I did what I usually do when confronted with a challenge – I said a quick, silent prayer. Believing I knew he was extorting money from people by his unauthorized actions, I decided to tell him I was a God fearing person whose holy book, the Bible, said what he was doing was wrong and I could not therefore in good conscience encourage him with payment. He did not like me saying that. Just then, an approaching VW Beetle attracted his attention and he moved to stop it. He went to its passenger window, exchanged a few words with the occupants, then reached his right hand into the car. When he stepped back, he came to me waving his ill-gotten gain, a paper bill, in my face. He barked, *"And I'm not going to do this! And I'm not going to do this!"* By saying it twice, he emphasized he thought I was crazy to think he should not do it. After all, wasn't the evidence justifying his doing it right there in his hand?  No, it wasn't, not so far as God is concerned.[1] "No," I said, "It is wrong for you to demand it, and it is wrong for them to give it to you."  Now he looked at me like a bull whose nose ring had just been pulled out.  Sounding like one too, he commanded me to leave.  Fortunately, though he motioned wildly, his hand was waving in the general direction of the airport.  Thank God, the freight was delivered at the expense of neither his *or* my conscience.[2]

*Lord, grant me wisdom to steer clear of questionable involvements.*

1) 1 Corinthians 6:10b

2) 2 Corinthians 4:2

*"As it is written: there is none righteous, no, not one."*

Here is a story that is sure to have your attention! A man gathered up his six month old boy, along with balloons, flowers, candy and card. It was a lot to juggle and, what with car seat and all, but he showed great patience, even making it to the car in just one trip. After carefully situating baby and things in the car, he drove off, excited about surprising his wife at her workplace for a celebration of her first Mother's Day. She, as well as her coworkers, was delighted and blessed by his thoughtful actions. Mission accomplished, he returned to the car for his trip home. The effort to pull off the surprise had left him exhausted, so nothing about getting back to the car seemed easy. Finally, after arranging things inside the car, he was back on the highway. Relaxing a little, he set his cruise control to a smooth 55 miles an hour when a peculiar thing happened. Passing drivers were flashing their lights and beeping their horns at him. What's that about? Just then, he realized... he had left the car seat on top of the car with his baby in it! In the next instant he heard a sound. It was the car seat with the baby in it, sliding off the roof, landing behind the car onto the highway! Mercifully, a driver following directly behind him had seen what was happening and had kept a safe distance, screeching to a halt in order to shield the baby from oncoming traffic. Having stopped in a panic, the father ran back, retrieved his unscathed child and, sobbing, returned to his car.

When the apostle Paul wrote of our weak, error ridden,

common humanity, he did not minimize its potential for negative consequence.  In fact, Paul reminds us we have each failed to get things right 100% of the time.[1]  We are like that good man who left his child on top of his car.  Except for one matter... our inability to do the right thing *did* result in a child's death.  That child, Paul says, was Jesus Christ.[2]

Our sins put Jesus in danger, but instead of headlights and horns, the heavenly Father only saw and heard an angry crowd yell, "Crucify him!  Crucify him!"  Unshielded from the cross, God's son, innocent and of perfect nature, died for an imperfect and fallen human race.  He did it so He might bring us to God.[3]

As believers, it is to our Father's credit that He doesn't leave us on top of our heavenly transport,[4] but places us safely inside His son for the duration of our journey.[5]  No falling off onto the highway for us![6]

*Lord, thank you for the safety and security I enjoy in you.*

1) Romans 3:23          4) John 14:6

2) Romans 5:8           5) 2 Corinthians 2:14

3) 1 Peter 3:18         6) Romans 8:35-39

*"Let us lay aside every weight,*

*and the sin which so easily ensnares us."*

I've had a few motorboats in my time. One thing I have learned, my boat in the water is a good thing, but water in my boat is not. A drain is located low on a boat stern, but one day I forgot to put the plug in it before launching. That meant water came into the boat before leaving the dock. The remedy, put the plug in and get the water out of the boat. Another time, upon launching, my son and his friends knocked a hole in a boat's fiberglass hull. Unaware they did it, they quickly lit out on the lake only to realize the boat was sinking faster than they could get the water out! They saw that the closest land was an island so they made for it, nearly beaching the boat before it submerged. Dad got an emergency call and, with great difficulty, we managed to re-float the boat and get it back home the same day. How much better it had been not to have water get inside the boat in the first place!

Christians in the world are a good thing. They are salt and light that helps others to know God. But the things of the world in Christians is not good. Like water in a boat, they weigh the believer down and have the potential to sink him. What are the things of the world? 1 John 2:16 tells us they are, "the lust of the flesh. The lust of the eyes, and the pride of life." These things have no place in a believer's life, just like water has no place in a boat.

Nonetheless, in the down and dirty of living in a broken world sometimes undesirable things leak into our lives. What to do? Well, what do we do once the water gets in the boat? We get it out! There is even a nautical term for it – bailing. It means to empty the boat of water by scooping it up with something and throwing it overboard. The water in the lake needs to stay in the lake . . . not in the boat!

Do you have some of the world's lust of the flesh, lust of the eyes, or pride of life in you? If you do, bail it out![1] Confess it! Throw it overboard! Forsake it. In so doing you will repair your leaks. Do it and you will run as designed, you will get where you want to go.[2]

*Lord, I do not want to harbor sin in my life.*

*Strengthen me to do the right thing and throw it overboard.*

1) Colossians 3:5-8

2) Colossians 3:9b-10

*"Now thanks be to God who always leads us in triumph in Christ, and through us diffuses the fragrance of His knowledge in every place."*

Years ago television viewers enjoyed a program entitled, "The A Team." The show's main characters were a few people of diverse personalities and backgrounds, talents and physical capacities. They would team up together to take on seemingly impossible jobs with a "git 'er done" attitudes. Their leader was a handsome, smart, charismatic, cigar chewing fellow who kept his team together, came up with the plans, and led in the team's deployment. In typical television plot fashion, the show's scripts were built around fantastic challenges to the team's success, yet they always managed to overcome and achieve their goals.

God has an "A Team" too. He has put people together to accomplish an incredible plan.[1] They are to go, make disciples of all nations, teaching them to obey all things Christ has commanded.[2] There has never been a more diverse people brought together for so singular a purpose. Their personalities, backgrounds, talents and physical differences equip them to "git 'er done," to go to every tongue, tribe and nation[3] whatever it takes.[4] Unlike the television show's leader, theirs passes on chewing the cigar. He is, however, not only smart, but within Him are all the treasures of wisdom and knowledge.[5] What's more, unlike the television's "A Team" leader, His charisma comes, not from His good looks,[6] but from what He is able to say and do.[7] The challenges God's "A Team" face would be unachieveable without Him,[8] but because God's man leads them the outcome of their combined sacrifice and efforts are guaranteed.[9]

God's "A Team" leader is His son, Jesus Christ. If you are not already on it, there is room for you on His team.[10] Ask Him, and he will receive, equip and lead you to have a fulfilling role in His unfolding plan to reach the world.

*Lord, I want a role on your team. Equip and lead me in the accomplishment of your will.*

1) John 15:16

2) Matthew 28:19, 20

3) Revelation 5:9

4) Titus 2:14

5) Colossians 2:2b, 3

6) Isaiah 53:2

7) Matthew 8:27

8) John 15:5

9) Matthew 16:18

10) John 6:37

**<u>Scar Stories</u>**

*"He was wounded for our transgressions, He was bruised for our iniquities; the chastisement for our peace was upon Him, and by His stripes we are healed."*

I have an early memory of being a little kid and playing with a toy gas station and cars. Back then, in the early 1950's, before all the plastic goods we enjoy today, toys were made of metal. Although they were durable, they were less safe. One day I cut my hand on the edge of the toy gas station garage door... today, at age 64, I still have the scar to prove it.

Most of us have scars and each of us has a story behind how we got them. Rural living Africans frequently tell of scars received from one of two things. The first is from the fact they do not have gas or electric power for cooking. They use wood fires and doing so gives occasion to burns on their hands and arms. The other scars they often have are on their legs or feet. These are from injury when using hand hoes while farming. Another people around the world who have similar common scars are the incarcerated. Frequent knife, bullet, and/or head wounds among them attest to the fact they experienced violence. Sad stories often accompany the scars of prisoners.

Jesus Christ had scars on his hands and feet. His scars were entirely like those of Africans, the incarcerated, or your own. Just like any of us, his human body produced pain and bled when injured. What does make his scars different from ours is that the injury which caused them, crucifixion, was for Him not unforeseen, no accident, not a chance occurrence.[1] "They pierced my hands and my feet,"[2] wrote the psalmist David 600 years before Christ was ever scarred. In fact, he wrote before there was a Roman Empire, before crucifixion had even been invented as a means of execution. David only wrote something so future as this by inspiration he received from the Holy Spirit.[3] Throughout his earth walk, Jesus knew and understood these things previously written about him.[4] He certainly was thinking of what David had written when He informed His disciples, "You know that after two days is the Passover, and the Son of Man will be delivered up to be crucified."[5]

Our scars came to us through unanticipated events, but Christ's was anticipated. He could have chosen to avoid His scars, yet did not.[6] Why? Not because suffering injury would be easy.[7] Consider His intense praying in the garden where He sweat drops of blood[8] and prayed, "Father, if it is possible, let this cup pass from me, nevertheless, not as I will, but as you will."[9] Christ knew the scar producing event He was giving himself over to endure[10] was going to be painful, and pain is never easy. Why then did He do it? He did it because of His love for us.[11] He did it to redeem us, to make a way for us to have eternal life by believing in Him.[12]

Yes, scars have stories behind them... and Christ's scars certainly have theirs.

*Lord, thank you for your willingness to suffer and be scarred for my sake.*

1) Acts 2:23

2) Psalm 22:16

3) 2 Peter 1:21

4) Luke 4:16-21

5) Matthew 26:2

6) Matthew 26:53

7.) Isaiah 52:14

8) Luke 22:44

9) Luke 22:42

10) Hebrews 12:2

11) John 3:16

12) John 11:25

*"Let a man examine himself."*

When managing the housekeeping department of a large hospital, my Regional Supervisor used to like to drop in to visit me unannounced. When He did, he always introduced his favorite thing to do by saying to me, "Let's take a walk." That was my cue to prepare to go on an inspection of the facility's rooms and corridors. At first glance, everywhere we went, our eyes met with recently buffed, shiny floors and neatly arranged rooms. No problems here, or so I would think. However, my supervisor's closer examination always managed to find something he wished to bring to my attention. It may have been some dust he fingered off a mirror edge, or that he found an accumulation of unswept "whatever" behind a habitually pinned back door. It also could have been materials shuffled off and out of place, perhaps hidden under a stairwell. The supervisor viewed things like these as reasons for correction, for increased vigilance in the attention required for good housekeeping.

At first, I thought my supervisor's critiquing unfair, even unduly harsh. Then, one day, he explained himself, he said, "I have found that if the small, out of order things are given proper attention, larger problems rarely ever develop. Train your housekeeping staff to do the small things and they will be less likely to fail in the larger concerns of good housekeeping."

As time has passed, I have grown in my appreciation of the

supervisor's good housekeeping principle. When I have permitted myself to "cut corners," to allow "little failures" in my spiritual life, it would eventually lead to larger neglect. For example, a little uncontrolled anger, unchecked, became words I should not have spoken and which could not be retrieved. Or, a couple of consecutive days of missed time with God, became longer periods of inattentiveness to God's Word and prayer.

Solomon wisely said, "It is the small foxes that spoil the vines."[1] Yes, little foxes... like not attending to accumulated spiritual dust behind the pinned back doors of our souls, or whatever is out of place under the stairwells of our minds.[2] These prevent us from the greater fruitfulness[3] that would please our supervisor and housekeeping inspector, the Holy Spirit.[4] It is He who often says to us, "Let's take a walk."[5]


*Lord, supervise me in inspecting my life for anything that needs to be changed.*


1) Song of Solomon 2:15

2) 2 Corinthians 7:1

3) John 15:8

4) 1 John 3:24

5) Galatians 5:16, 25

# *Works by L. R. Abbott*

## ONE MAN'S JOURNEY

What does a Christian life look like?  The author offers his own up in example. Not that his life is just like yours, but the spiritual truths God teaches him apply to your journey.  Come with him on a pilgrimage reminiscent of the one made by Pilgrim, the main character in John Bunyan's immortal classic Pilgrim's Progress. On the way to the Celestial City, Pilgrim did not avoid every pitfall, and neither did the author.  What about you?  Have you ever strayed, ever failed to stay on the right path?  Confirm you are on the right path. Find strength for your pilgrimage and get to where you want to arrive... read One Man's Journey.

## THE MONTH THAT MATTERS SERIES

### A MONTH THAT MATTERS

### ANOTHER MONTH THAT MATTERS

### ONE MORE MONTH THAT MATTERS

If you enjoyed this volume of A Month That Matters, you will also enjoy the other volumes of evangelical essays and prayers written for your heart and mind.  Each presents a unique set of writings, one for each day of the month.  None are too long not to be read in one sitting, but none is too short to be shallow. Take yourself out of yourself for a few minutes each day and read more of the Month That Matters series... you will be glad you did.

# ABOUT THE AUTHOR

L. R. Abbott's secular studies earned him a B.S. In Sociology with a minor in English. To prepare for teaching Sociology in colleges he attended graduate school at the New School for Social Research in New York City. There, disillusioned with his search for the answer to life's meaning, he quit his studies and became a practioner and advocate of Transcendental Meditation. Eventually he met Christ and nothing was the same. In the ensuing years his hunger for spiritual knowledge led him to attend, or complete by extension, classes and courses from Moody Bible Institute, Philadelphia College of the Bible, the Central Jersey Bible Institute and Columbia International University. Now retired, he lives in Columbia, South Carolina.

The author may be contacted at OMJAbbott@yahoo.com

Made in the USA
Middletown, DE
12 July 2017